WE MUST DEFEND AMERICA
and
Put an End to MADness

Daniel O. Graham

Regnery Gateway
Chicago

Reprinted by Conservative Press, Inc., P.O. Box 1430, Falls Church, VA 22041 by
special arrangement with Regnery Gateway, Inc., 360 W. Superior Street, Chicago,
IL 60610-0890

CONTENTS

CONTENTS

FOREWORD
William L. Armstrong
United States Senator

This small book is important.

General Graham and his team of scientists, engineers, and strategists of Project High Frontier have gone to the heart of the national security debates that seem to swirl endlessly and fruitlessly around the nation's Capitol. Behind demands for unilateral disarmament or nuclear freeze or for massive increases in defense expenditures lies a commonly held concern that American strategy for avoiding nuclear war is not working. Some Americans argue that the problem is inadequate efforts in arms-control, others point to inadequate attention to the arming of our forces. High Frontier clearly identifies the real culprit—bad strategy.

Those who feel there is no option but to support nuclear "freeze" and those who feel obliged to support all options for increased

5

offensive nuclear strength may be amazed to learn (and perhaps refuse to believe) that they share common ground. Both views are rooted in the mind-sets created by the theory of Mutual Assured Destruction, a doctrine which has, for two decades, fundamentally influenced the shape, size, and nature of our strategic forces and held sway over our attempts to reach arms-control agreements with the Soviets. While antagonists from both sides in the debate over national security have from time to time denounced MAD as a doctrine, they seem to accept it as a sort of "immutable law of nature." Both sides tend to argue for a perpetual balance-of-terror, with one side willing to leave that balance right where it is despite Soviet advantages, the other demanding a better balance through increases in the U.S. nuclear arsenal.

The MAD doctrine was formulated in the mid-60s on the assumption that once the Soviet Union had acquired our then extant capability to absorb a first strike and still launch a retaliatory blow capable of wholesale slaughter of the civilian population, the Kremlin would then sign an agreement formalizing this war-deterring balance-of-terror at some level acceptable to both sides. A vital corollary to this doctrine was the contention that any defense of either population against the

6

effects of nuclear weapons would be "destabilizing" since it would tend to remove them from the hostage status on which the deterrent rested fundamentally. As Mr. John Newhouse, a strong proponent of the MAD doctrine, wrote in 1973 in his book, COLD DAWN: THE STORY OF SALT: "Offense is defense, defense is offense. Killing people is good, killing weapons is bad."

In 1983, we could look back on the origins of MAD and chastise its authors as bloodthirsty fools. But that was not the case. In the mid-60s, there was an even more fundamental and more widely held assumption underpinning the MAD doctrine. This was the assumption that the offensive nuclear weapon, especially in the form of the long-range ballistic missile, would dominate military affairs forever. Only the strategic *offense* was worth considering, because no strategic *defensive* system could ever become practicable, except perhaps as a limited protection for offensive weapons. Strategic defense of the population was deemed unachievable. Such an assumption flies in the face of the history of military technology which has seen the dominance of defense or offense shift back and forth in an almost predictable rhythm. But the fact is that most Americans in the earlier years of the nuclear age accepted the absolute nature of the offensive nuclear weapon and MAD was the result.

In any case, searching for fools or villains of the past in the clear vision of hindsight is somewhat unfair and certainly fruitless. What is needed now is to understand why MAD has not worked and what can be done about it. This is the major theme of this book.

General Graham points out clearly why MAD has been a catastrophic failure. Some would argue with him on the grounds that we have not had a nuclear war during the twenty years of MAD. Superficially, that sounds like a good point, but *only* superficially. U.S. adherence to MAD and Soviet rejection of that theory have resulted in a Soviet capability to wreak far greater destruction on us that we could cause in retaliation. None have ever argued that as soon as the Soviets had achieved such capabilities they would *attack* us. What *has* been argued is that superior nuclear power in the hands of the Soviets make such an attack more likely and their behavior more aggressive. *These* baneful effects of our failed strategy are amply evident. Americans who ten years ago thought the chances of nuclear war extremely remote, now see it as much more likely—and they are unfortunately correct. Soviet invasion of Afghanistan and their blatant disregard for international agreements in the use of chemical-biological weapons against the people of Afghanistan and Laos is ample proof of increased aggressiveness. *These* are the real fruits of our adhering to MAD and thus allowing a dangerous imbalance of power to accrue to the favor of the Soviet Union.

General Graham also makes the case convincingly that the assumptions underlying MAD have been destroyed by U.S. technological advances. He points out that our advantages in space technology can provide a non-nuclear shield against the long-range nuclear missile which MAD considers the "ultimate weapon." While some may argue that High Frontier will cost more or take longer to achieve than the General believes, or that there are better technological solutions to the problem of strategic defense of America, none can argue persuasively that it *cannot be done*.

I agree with General Graham that, once a new national strategy along the lines of High Frontier is adopted, the bureaucratic opposition on technical and costing grounds will quickly disappear. I also agree that a straightforward commitment to the use of space for our security *and* our economic growth, as this book advocates, will energize the critical high technology sector of the U.S. economy to our great benefit.

Yes, this small book is important. Its premises may become the focus of a new and more fruitful national debate over security issues. I hope that the potential participants in that debate, whether in government or in the general public, read and understand what is said herein.

Senator William L. Armstrong

I.
The Shades of the Past

*"Those who cannot remember the past
are condemned to fulfill it."*
–George Santayana

We are witnessing an eerie and tragic repetition of history. The United States, today's leader of the opposition to the powerful totalitarian communist system, is following the footsteps of Great Britain, yesteryear's leader of the opposition to Nazism. The stench of appeasement, pacifism, self-flagellation, and abandonment of principle hangs heavy over our land. A mulelike refusal to face reality threatens the existence of free societies everywhere. A mindless terror of war brings us ever-closer to war while decisions calculated to increase U.S. weakness only encourage foreign aggression. Many American intellectuals and politicians today are echoing the plaints of intellectuals and politicians in pre-World War II Britain: "Peace in our time, no matter the price."

11

Both history and nature provide the unmistakable lesson that aggressors do not attack those who are willing and able to defend themselves. Switzerland has lived in peace for centuries, peaceful but not pacifist. Every able-bodied Swiss from age eighteen until age fifty-five is ever-ready to take arms in defense of his country. It is weakness and pacifism that bring on war. The politics of appeasement and disarmament, now unleashed in America, moves us always closer to World War III as those same politics in Britain encouraged Hitler to launch World War II.

A recent public television series, "Churchill, The Wilderness Years," eloquently documents the self-delusion of Neville Chamberlain, Stanley Baldwin, and Lord Halifax, Britain's appeasement-minded leaders in the 1930s. These men blundered down the road to World War II, using precisely the same arguments of today's liberals, suppressing Churchill's warnings and side-kicking demands from the great majority of Englishmen for improved defenses.

When Churchill warned that Hitler was out to conquer the world, the appeasers scoffed. They called him a "warmonger" and "militarist." In fact, believe it or not, British politicians were convinced that, with Hitler, agreements could be reached which would divide the world between Britain and Germany. This included taking African colonies away from other countries, such as Portugal, and handing them over to Hitler. These appeasement leaders become perpetual apologists for Nazi Germany, drinking much champagne with Nazi leaders and striving mightily to stifle news of Nazi barbarism.

When Churchill and the military leadership demanded repair of Britain's defenses, Baldwin and Chamberlain countered with arguments that such action was "provocative and destabilizing," that "increased defense spending would hurt domestic social programs," and that the small British heavy bomber force was an "adequate deterrent." When the British public demanded more attention to defense, Baldwin and Chamberlain made public pronouncements of intent to strengthen armed forces while privately continuing to whittle them down.

The pre-World War II leaders in Britain were, in addition, devotees of arms control agreements, determined not to entertain evidence that arms-control was indeed failing. The major arms control agreement of the day, the London Naval Agreement, specified how many of what type of warships the major powers might have. The great advantage of the treaty to the Baldwins and Chamberlains of the day was the rationale it provided for dismantling older ships of the British Navy and not building new ones.

The extremes to which this devotion to arms control led the British government are astonishing. In the mid-thirties, for example, British Naval Intelligence discovered the battleship *Bismarck* under construction in a German shipyard and duly reported it to Baldwin's government. Its tonnage made it an obvious violation of the London Agreement, a fact which the government could not bring itself to accept. Under detailed questioning, the intelligence officers agreed that they had seen only the upper parts of the *Bismarck*, not the lower. When asked whether the *Bismarck* would violate the tonnage restrictions of the London Naval Agreement if the ship turned out to actually have a flat bottom, the officers had to admit it would not. The Baldwin government maintained then that the *Bismarck* was not a violation of arms-control and that everyone, in fact, should be pleased that Germany was abiding by its treaties and building a large warship with a flat bottom. The *Bismarck*, they said, was obviously designed to pass through the Kiel Canal to the Baltic where it could only be used against the Soviet Union—but no, not against Britain.

Later, thousands of British sailors lost their lives to the world's most formidable battleship, the *Bismarck*.

As late as 1937, in the face of massive arms buildup by Nazi Germany, Chamberlain still opined that arms-control agreements could be reached with Hitler and that such agreements would indeed avert war.

Pre-war Britain was riddled with pacifism. Vast numbers of young men joined the Oxford Movement which demanded of its adherents a sworn statement never to bear arms for their country in any circumstances. This phenomenal extreme of pacifism spread quickly to the United States.

Pacifists terrorized the British populace with "end-of-the-world" scenarios for any future war. The agents of apocalypse then were not, of course, nuclear weapons, but chemical and biological warfare, the horrors of which were portrayed by film and theater, espoused in pamphlets and on radio, and even appeared in the art and literature of the day.

One need not be a historian to realize the disturbing similarities between pre-war Britain and America today. In the face of an even more powerful totalitarian state with even more clearly stated goals of world domination, American politicians and intellectuals pursue the same arguments and policies which tempted the aggressor to strike Britain in 1939.

It is indeed tragic that World War II and its destruction of 41 million people could have been averted had Western democracies paid heed to Churchill. The German General Staff was prepared to oust Hitler from power had Great Britain and France showed the slightest symptoms of a backbone in the face of Hitler's aggressions. Instead, they demonstrated a foolhardy willingness to trust their nation's futures to paper scraps signed by the leader of the Third Reich, and, as particularly in the case of the infamous Munich Agreement, they convinced the tyrant and the Germans in general that the Nazi Fuhrer could pursue his grand designs unimpeded.

Though Churchill was ignored, his persistence forced the bare minimum of action required to avoid the defeat of Great Britain after his parliamentary opponents had finally blundered their way into war.

In an action so typical of today's U.S. bureaucracy, Churchill's troublesome demands for strengthened British defenses were turned over to a committee—no doubt in the hope they would be "studied to death."

The Air Defense Research Committee was established by the British government to look at the prospects for defending Britain from the formidable Luftwaffe. The question was whether the Royal Air Force should allocate funds to a "retaliatory" bomber force, or instead should build up a homeland defense force of Spitfire or Hawker Hurricane interceptors, as well as radars and civil defenses. The threat of annihilation perceived by the British at that time is tantamount to our own present perceptions of nuclear ballistic missiles. The British anticipated the Luftwaffe to make heavy use not only of incendiaries but also of gas bombs. This threat some held, was impossible to defend against with available or foreseeable technology. Fortunately for the Western democracies, the British government came down on the side of defending Great Britian—the interceptor force, the air raid wardens, and the radars that won the Battle of Britain. Unlike the American government of thirty years later, it did not embark on a wholesale ideological policy excursion in the direction of mandatory homeland vulnerability.

Luckily for Britain and the Free World, Britain was spared from direct attack, in the early stages of the war, by eight months of "phony" war and by Hitler's need to finish off Poland, France, and the Low Countries. This gave Britain enough time to put Churchill in charge and produce just barely enough Spitfires, radars, and other defenses to win the Battle of Britain. And, very luckily for Britain, American democracy and an untouched American arsenal was ready and available to provide the sinew of British resistance.

Such luck will hardly be in evidence if America does not pay attention to its present day Churchills. America must listen earlier. World War III must and can be prevented, as World War II could have been, by making it rivetingly clear to any potential aggressor that war or any threat of war stands no chance of success. Such as they are, modern weapons would not permit us time to repair or complete our defenses after a war commences, and certainly there will be no arsenal of democracy somewhere in the world to offer us assistance.

Today we are indeed marching toward World War III under the old and familiar banner of "Peace in our Time." But instead, America must be defended.

II.
The Problem

*"There are none so blind
as those who will not see."
–Jeremiah*

In the field of national security, the appellation "conservative" is applied to Americans in both political parties who see a clear and present military threat from Left totalitarians led by an aggressive Soviet Union. Among Republicans, this view is simply called "conservative"; among Democrats, "neo-conservative." Senator Jesse Helms is typical of Republican conservatives; the late Senator Henry M. "Scoop" Jackson of Democrats. Though these men have serious disagreements on a broad range of political issues, both are opposed to the weakening of U.S. defenses and to such flawed arms-control treaties as SALT II. These men clearly are among the Churchills of our time.

They are opposed by politicians in both parties who echo the 1930s arguments of

19

Baldwin and Neville Chamberlain against Churchill. Such view points have come to be called "liberal" even though their stance demands toleration, if not outright appeasement, of the most oppressive regimes.

The division between "Churchills" and "Chamberlains" of U.S. politics is a division between realists and wishful thinkers. Essentially the split is one between those who are willing to bet America's future on the trustworthiness of the Soviets and those who are not. While the peace-through-trust school enjoys the support of America's intellectuals and its media, the peace-through-strength school has the overwhelming support of average Americans, ample proof of which is the total rejection of George McGovern in 1976 and the rout of dovish senators and representatives in the 1978 and 1980 elections.

The ordinary American is not a simple-minded jingoist when he makes his choice against the politics of weakness propounded by the Left and when he ignores the anti-defense bombardments from the media. He wisely refuses to accept national security solutions which require him to trust the Soviet Union. He may be beguiled briefly by disarmament schemes and "nuclear freeze," but as soon as he perceives their abject reliance on goodwill and trustworthiness on the part of the Kremlin, he balks.

To sell their solutions, solutions totally dependent upon the cooperation of the Soviets, the Left spokesmen are saddled with the requirement to convince others that the Soviet Union is trustworthy. They must, therefore, strive to create a "climate of trust" in which they must constantly excuse Soviet behavior. The horrors of communist totalitarianism such as genocide in Cambodia, the "boat people" of Vietnam, the Yellow Rain of poisonous chemicals and biological agents on defenseless people, the suppression of Poland and invasion of Afghanistan, and the deliberate destruction of 40 million Soviet citizens must be hidden from public view or explained away lest they endanger creation of a "climate of trust." The relentless Soviet build-up of nuclear attack forces must be ignored or described as mere defensive reaction to the wickedness of the United States—particularly that of "warmongering" Americans who support a strong defense. Thus do the more avid spokesmen for arms-control and nuclear freeze become perpetual apologists for the most vicious totalitarians and warmongers of modern history and constant attackers of the United States and its institutions.

Of course such views are applauded and supported by the Kremlin. Would we not support and applaud some mass movement among Russians which constantly painted the

21

United States in the best possible light and condemned the Soviet regime? Still, nuclear freeze advocates scream "McCarthyism!" whenever anyone notes they are eagerly supported by the Soviet Union. The truth they will not admit is that the Soviet Union readily acknowledges its role in Western pacifist movements while squelching any such activity within its own empire.

We speak here of the leadership of the disarmament and nuclear-freeze movements, not of the rank and file American. Many Americans, quite simply, terrorized by grossly exaggerated scenarios of nuclear death and destruction, have been led, in desperation, to support the pacifist Left. This phenomenon is due to more than mere naivete.

Much of the emotion that today swirls around nuclear issues stems from the ill-considered decision of a generation ago not to build any defensive systems. It is time to re-evaluate that old decision in light of the many technical advances and other changes since then.

To abandon all our strategic defenses as well as let up on all efforts to generate new ones—as we actually did over the past twenty years—was nothing short of foolhardy. Such an error, Soviet leadership would never make, and never did. In view of the high potential payoffs, we should have put top priority on developing as soon as possible the best anti-ballistic missile defensive systems that science and money could produce.

Had we done so, success would have brought great benefits in strengthened Western courage and resolve as well as in more effective means to deal with the Soviets on nuclear issues. We still can earn such benefits *if:*

—we dispel myths and attitudes which have blinded us to fundamental facts for a full generation;

—we look at what defense technology can do for us right now if properly applied;

—and finally, if we recognize the psychological and political payoffs inherent in a ballistic missile defense system that offers us hope just by its presence.

This will enable us to depart from depending upon a balance of terror invoking visions of indescribable disasters for everyone, which is all that our present sole emphasis on offensive forces seems to offer.

Perhaps, the most damaging of all oversights in the past twenty years has been the failure to appreciate the real payoff of defensive systems in the nuclear age—that of destroying the aggressor's confidence in any of his own nuclear attack plans. If an aggressor must first penetrate a defensive system, he cannot possibly anticipate how many, which ones, or whether his weapons will explode where intended. He can have little idea of the possible effects of his own nuclear attack, and thus cannot afford to take chances when the consequences of failure are so great. Thus, defense is essential to effective long-lasting deterrence.

For a generation, we have failed to comprehend the disastrous psychological consequences of a nation and a Western world absolutely naked to nuclear attacks. The human mind will not long endure any hopeless situation. It must turn, in self-defense and desperation, to denial and self-delusion in order to generate at least some crumbs of hope. When a sense of hopelessness combines with the terror which overwhelms many individuals at the thought of any nuclear hostilities, the political consequences are almost wholly unpredictable. Hence, the many anti-nuclear proposals and movements so rife today in Europe and America and which play directly into Soviet hands.

If the people of this country and of our allies were defended from nuclear attack, they would no longer be stampeded by their nuclear fears into support for ill-reasoned propositions based upon the forlorn hope that the Soviets share their paralyzing anxieties. The ultimate folly would be an unthinking rush toward expensive repairs in the current inadequate strategy without a reasoned examination of alternate strategies. Such alternative strategies, actually, are increasingly feasible technically and would rely upon the present U.S. superiority in space technology. The attitudes of the past two decades must be washed out or else we will miss the enormous strategic opportunity offered by our unrivalled technology.

III.
A Course of Action

*"Righteous indignation is no substitute
for a good course of action."*
— *Otto von Bismarck*

Concerned Americans of both political parties and all sectors of society have inveighed against the dangerous shift of military power from the Western Alliance to the Soviet Empire. A great deal of righteous indignation has been aired, and well-founded indignation it has been. The Soviet Union, emboldened by its evermore dominant military superiority, suppresses the Poles, invades Afghanistan, violates treaties, and sets up communist regimes by force in our own backyard of Central America. Their build-up of accurate long-range ballistic missiles threatens the continued existence of our nation. Yes, indeed, there is ample cause for righteous indignation.

But Bismarck's words are as true today as they were when spoken. More must be presented to the American public than indignation. We must present a course of action which will correct the problem. Such action must make sense to ourselves, our fellow Americans, and to free people everywhere. We must offer a course of action which insures U.S. security *without* reliance on Soviet cooperation and one which will be understood and supported by all ordinary Americans.

This is where High Frontier comes in.

High Frontier is a comprehensive, new U.S. national strategy; it addresses not only our security problems, but also economic, political, and moral issues facing the nation. If adopted, High Frontier would accomplish the following:

—Replace the failed and morally suspect doctrine of Mutual Assured Destruction (MAD) with a strategy of Assured Survival;

—Effectively close the "window of vulnerability" by denying the Soviets a nuclear first strike capability—without deploying one more U.S. nuclear weapon;

—Create a reliable effective deterrent to nuclear war by defending the United States and the Free World rather than by threatening a suicidal punitive strike at Soviet civilians;

—Create an immediate surge in the high-technology sector of the U.S. economy by opening and securing space for private enterprise;

—Provide positive and challenging goals for American youth and a restored image of U.S. success and leadership abroad.

—Do all of the above at costs to the taxpayer below all other available alternatives to meet the current Soviet threat;

—And do so with or without Soviet cooperation.

This, I realize, is a pretty heady set of claims for the High Frontier strategic concepts. Certainly, this list of advantages raises the skeptical eyebrow and the proper question: "If these results can be attained, why isn't High Frontier already national policy?" The answer to that question is sad but simple: High Frontier encounters severe bureaucratic and ideological resistance—both based primarily upon determination to perpetuate the failed and immoral doctrine of Mutual Assured Destruction and, secondarily, on the bog of red tape which has become a normality in U.S. exploitation of technology. Allow me to support these claims.

High Frontier is the result of prodigious efforts in 1981 and 1982 by a strong team of scientists, engineers, strategists, and economists supported by private donations. Their objective has been to find a means to end-run the Soviet nuclear threat with U.S. technology. The search for a clear-cut technological advantage over the Soviet Union led inexorably to space where our advantages include the transportation system, the Shuttle. The Soviets trail us in space transport by eight to ten years. Another obvious advantage is in miniaturization, the ability to make things small, light, and efficient. Because of it, every pound we put into space does five or six times as much useful work as a pound put into space by the Soviets. These advantages are not merely additive, they are compounding. Since the limiting factor in exploiting space is the cost-per-pound to orbit, this combination of superior U.S. technology allows us a fundamental advantage over the Soviets.

The High Frontier team determined that this advantage could best be exploited by providing a layered strategic defense to nullify the Soviet threat of a first strike. Somewhat to our surprise, we found that an effective spaceborne defense could be had in five to six years using off-the-shelf technology and that emerging technology could greatly strengthen the first layer of strategic defense in ten to twelve years. In addition, we found there were relatively inexpensive and quick options available in point-defense systems to protect the U.S. deterrent on the ground and thus deny the Soviets a first strike capability while the first spaceborne system was being deployed. None of these systems require any nuclear weapons. Nor do they even require lasers or other beam weapons, although such weaponry might figure prominently in the second-stage defense layer in ten to twelve years.

High Frontier was launched as a search for national security solutions, but we found that the core space technology required for such solutions was the same technology necessary to open up space for private enterprise to tap its limitless sources of material and energy. Furthermore, the unique environment of space—zero gravity, vacuum, perfectly sterile conditions, and unlimited heat sink— provides opportunities for the manufacture of products impossible on Earth. It became clear to the High Frontier team that U.S. commercial and military uses of space would proceed in tandem, just as in earlier centuries the merchantman and man-of-war developed side by side, making maximum use of the high seas and producing some hundred years of Pax Britannica.

Thus were the concepts High Frontier developed. High Frontier is a call for a new strategic direction. It is not merely a list of attractive civil and military technical recommendations.

High Frontier very early identified the things that must be done—the urgent requirements that must be met—in order to gain the sought-after strategic goals. To illustrate the feasibility of meeting these requirements, we selected, from the many available options, four military and four civilian programs which had been proposed by aerospace companies or independent engineers—programs which could stand scrutiny for technology, costs, and timing. At this point, there was opposition within the High Frontier team. Some felt the illustrative systems would be attacked in great detail by naysayers to avoid consideration of High Frontier's basic strategic recommendations. The majority of the team, while agreeing to that probability, felt that, without describing hardware programs which could support the strategic thrust of High Frontier, the entire idea would be ignored along with the hundreds of other strategy treatises gathering bookshelf dust.

The pessimists were proved at least partly correct. The first vigorous opposition to High Frontier came in an assault on one of our eight illustrative programs—the first layer of spaceborne defense, which we called Global Ballistic Missile Defense I. The other military systems have thus far drawn relatively little attack and the four civil programs practically none.

The disputed program, GBMD I, comprises a large number of orbiting satellites (432 to be exact) each of which carries forty or fifty small rockets capable of intercepting up to eighty percent of a Soviet long-range missile attack early in trajectory. It utilizes almost entirely off-the-shelf technology and can be acquired in five or six years at an estimated cost of $15 billion. This system is, of course, conceptual, not an optimized engineering proposal. Criticisms of GBMD I have ranged from the wild to the reasonable.

Early on, High Frontier's GBMD was assailed as "defying the laws of physics" and posing costs of up to $400 billion. Such criticisms were among other broad expressions of doubt as to the competency and even honesty of our team which came mostly from bureaucrats, obvious guarders of the turf, and were not difficult to counter. In addition to the expected not-invented-here syndrome, the assault on High Frontier was reinforced by the inescapable fact that its recommended actions ran directly counter to such presumably important ongoing Department of Defense programs as MX-MPS (Race Track) and Dense Pack.

Anti-High Frontier polemics subsided by mid-1982 since too many credible sources supported the basic technical soundness of our proposals. Chief among such supporters was Boeing Aerospace Company which, quite unbeknownst to us, scrubbed down our technology with some of their best engineering talent and declared it feasible although they disagreed with us on the details. Today, the bureaucratic response has been softened, standardized into a "yes, but..." answer to all queries. And, a lot of queries are being received as the public hears more of High Frontier. "Yes, High Frontier's strategy of Assured Survival is supported by the Administration, *but* we believe the costs of space-borne defense and the time required to acquire it have been seriously underestimated..." etc.

At this juncture, government decision-makers should consider some recent history.

In 1956, President Dwight D. Eisenhower was briefed by a Navy team on a rather ambitious concept for strengthening the U.S. nuclear deterrent. These bold fellows thought we could build a very large nuclear-powered submarine that could launch ballistic missiles from under the water and we could devise a means for the submarine to know its position well enough for missiles to very accurately hit intended targets in the Soviet Union. Eisenhower saw the enormous strategic advantages of such a craft and, despite numerous serious technological unknowns, ordered it built. At that time, most of the U.S. Navy thought either that such a system could not or should not be built. Nonetheless, less than four years later, the first Polaris submarine put out to sea.

In 1959, as the space age was dawning, Eisenhower recognized the enormous advantages of using our advanced technology for defense against long-range Soviet ballistic missiles. He ordered the Pentagon to conduct urgent, all-out research to determine the feasibility of defending the United States against such missiles. Mind you, this was *before* the Soviets *or* the United States had deployed the first intercontinental ballistic missile (ICBM).

The Department of Defense responded vigorously in an effort named Project Defender. By mid-1962, this highly competent group of Department of Defense scientists and engineers had concluded that the United States could deploy a non-nuclear spaceborne defense capable of stopping up to ninety-percent of a Soviet missile attack, and, could accomplish this within six years of a go-ahead decision, utilizing technology then available or confidently expected to be.

Twenty years later, a group of scientists, engineers, and strategists collectively known as Project High Frontier, came to the same conclusion. Armed with data which had not been available to President Eisenhower's group—numbers, locations, and characteristics of Soviet long-range missiles—and supported by dramatic advances in almost every technology pertinent to the problem, they concluded that indeed the United States and its allies in the Free World could be protected from a Soviet nuclear missile strike with a non-nuclear spaceborne defensive system in five or six years and at reasonable cost.

This bit of history should evoke some disturbing questions. How could Eisenhower order Polaris submarines to be built, an effort fraught with enormous technical uncertainties, and get an "Aye-aye, sir" from the Navy and concrete results in less than four years? How could President Kennedy, a few years later, order a manned landing on the moon—a project also involving serious technical unknowns—and get concrete results in seven years? And why is it that, today, a system such as the Global Ballistic Missile Defense system of High Frontier—based primarily on twenty-year-old technology—can be opposed on the grounds of technical problems, long lead times and cost? Has the United States over the past twenty years become technologically inept? And why is it that a concept such as High Frontier had to come from a privately financed, non-governmental effort outside the complex of buyers and suppliers of military hardware?

There are many correct and partially correct answers to these questions, too many to cover in detail here. However, they are all rooted primarily in adherence to bad strategy.

The bad strategy is Mutual Assured Destruction, although "strategy" is an unduly flattering term to apply to this odd theory. MAD holds that U.S. security and the avoidance of nuclear war are entirely dependent on the maintenance of a balance of terror in which both the United States and the Soviet Union can absorb a nuclear first strike and still be able to wreak such terrible vengeance that neither side will ever use nuclear weapons. One vital corollary of MAD is that both sides must refrain from defending their citizens because to protect them would deny or ameliorate the terribleness of vengeance and would therefore be "destabilizing."

Another little understood corollary of MAD is its fundamental dependence on arms control. The entire concept is dependent upon agreements on both sides to keep the balance-of-terror balanced. Without an agreement with the Soviets as to just how many of what types of nuclear weapons each side should have, the pressure to add more and better offensive systems is inexorable. MAD without SALT (or START) dictates that each side must keep adding offensive weapons because each is dependent upon the surviving fraction of its nuclear force after a first strike by the opponent. This fraction diminishes steadily because of technical improvements to offensive weaponry. Weapon totals must therefore be periodically increased to insure that adequate numbers survive. One literally adds offensive weapons to be destroyed in a first strike.

Thus MAD comes in a package along with avoidance of strategic defense and a large bag of SALT. Remove any ingredient and the entire doctrine collapses. This accounts for the paradoxical tacit alliance among adamant arms control enthusiasts and the offense-only school of thought. The nuclear-freeze, unilateral disarmament cabal finds it most useful to support MAD since it demands that the American people remain defenseless in the face of their visions of nuclear apocalypse. So long as they can make a case for their slogan: "There is No Defense!" they can drive terrified citizens into their political fold. The offense-only school of thought supports MAD for entirely different purposes, dreading the thought of an effective strategic defense which would compete for resources with offensive systems. It reminds one of the once common support of Dry Laws in parts of the country rampant with both bootleggers and the Women's Christian Temperance Union. Both sides supported Prohibition but for quite separate reasons: bootleggers wanted to sell liquor and the WCTU wanted to stamp it out with legalisms.

In reality, despite fifteen years of American adherence, MAD was doomed from the start. Its only chance for success lay in the hope that the Soviets would adopt the same doctrine. They did not. They labeled it "bourgeois naivete"—which indeed it is—and proceeded to work for a war-winning nuclear advantage. They did not eschew strategic defenses. They have spent about one ruble on strategic defense for every ruble spent on strategic offense. By contrast, the U.S. has spent one dollar on strategic defense for every $10,000 spent on strategic offense. The Soviets did not couple their SALT positions to MAD as we have, but instead insured that SALT negotiations did not stand in the way of their drive for a war-winning superiority.

Our adherence to MAD has produced a grossly unstable and dangerous strategic situation resembling the classic Western movie scene where two men face each other down on Main Street, each waiting for the other to go for his gun, each knowing that the man who gets in the first shot has by far the better chance for survival. What is worse, the Soviet gunman stands behind a partial barrier of strategic defense while the American stands unprotected.

This strange doctrine of MAD, denied from time to time by our political and military leaders alike, still underpins the shape of our forces, the nature of new system proposals (e.g., MX-Racetrack and Dense Pack) and our approach to arms-control. This is the primary reason we seem unable to make the bold moves to insure our security that we could make in Eisenhower's day. It is also the prime reason ordinary Americans view Washington arguments over the defense budget and the billions necessary for deploying the MX missile as a sort of MADness. For it is.

IV.
The High Frontier Military Program

*"If a strong man shall keep
his court well-guarded,
he shall live in peace."*
—St. Luke

Almost two decades of adherence to unsound theories and bad strategy has led the United States and its Free World allies to a crisis in our security. Ten years ago the United States was so militarily strong that an attack on our homeland was considered nearly inconceivable by not only ourselves but by friend and foe alike. We were simply too strong to be attacked or intimidated. This is no longer the case.

Today, Americans feel threatened by the possibility of nuclear attack, some so keenly that they grasp at such desperate measures as "nuclear freeze" in the vain hope that mere expression of those fears will remove the threat. Our allies no longer feel confident that American strategic power is sufficient to permit them to withstand the blandishments and threats emanating from the Kremlin. And, Soviets themselves grow ever bolder in flexing the sinews of their vast armies, fleets, and nuclear attack forces—secure in the knowledge that American nakedness to attack by their massive array of long-range missiles ensures American timidity.

Daily, this basic situation grows worse. It must be corrected as quickly and effectively as American ingenuity and productive capacity will allow. Otherwise, the adverse trends in Free World security will become irrevocable; liberty will either flicker out slowly as we yield gradually, or die in a blinding flash of nuclear war.

We could once again recite the doleful numbers showing the Soviet Empire's advantages over the West in divisions, planes, tanks, ships, nuclear missiles, bombers, submarines, and megatons in their nuclear arsenal. Only one set of figures suffices to demonstrate the most critical U.S. disadvantage in military power: Should the Soviets launch an all out nuclear attack on the United States, the number of Americans killed instantly is likely to be 150 to 160 million. If we then retaliated with all surviving U.S. nuclear forces, the number of Soviet citizens likely to be killed instantly is ten to twenty million. These are not figures derived by some group of enthusiasts for greater U.S. defense spending, but official computations by the Carter Administration.

No American would contemplate the loss of ten to twenty million people as an acceptable price for destroying a political obstacle. But we must remember that ten to twenty million is fewer than the Soviets lost in World War II, and a third to a half of the number of Soviet citizens liquidated by the Communist Party for inadequate ardor in support of their regime. No U.S. military task is half so important as changing these awesome figures and thus deterring such carnage.

One approach would be to quickly and sharply increase U.S. offensive nuclear strength to the point where we could confidently expect to slaughter an additional 100 million Soviets in retaliation. This could conceivably get the balance of terror back in balance. It would mean, of course, that we would have to build far more missiles and bombers than actually needed to carry out such a task, since we would surely lose many in a Soviet first strike.

Another approach which can insure a greater slaughter on the Soviet side is to put all nuclear attack forces on hair-trigger and aim all at Soviet population centers. This would mean discarding our policy of accepting a first blow before retaliation and discarding any pretense that our weapons are aimed at military targets. If our intelligence and warning systems indicated that a Soviet attack had been launched or was about to be, we could fire away at their cities.

The other option is to address the other side of the equation—the utter vulnerability of the United States which would result in 150 million deaths, a literal destruction of the nation. If we can assure the survival of the United States and remove the temptation to deliver a knock-out blow, surely the likelihood of nuclear war can be sharply reduced.

There are also two ways to approach the problems of protecting the American people from nuclear annihilation—"damage-limiting," as it has sometimes arisen in Pentagon jargon. One is to design counterforce weapons capable of destroying Soviet weapons before they can be launched against us. Such weapons can be highly effective in reducing the weight of an adversary's nuclear attack. But their effectiveness is heavily dependent upon getting in the first blow—preemption or first strike. This, in fact, is one of the ways the Soviets have created the gross imbalance in damage likely to be sustained by either side in a nuclear exchange. They have concentrated their efforts on large, accurate, quick-acting weapons such as their 300-plus SS-18 ICBMs which alone threaten to destroy the U.S. deterrent force on the ground. Both Soviet military pronouncements and their weapons programs clearly prove their intention to deliver the first blow in any nuclear war. We could, of course, go the same route to reduce damage to the United States. However, it is most unlikely that the political ethos of this country would ever allow a basic strategy of preemption or first strike.

Counterforce weaponry makes imminently more military and moral sense than countervalue or "city-busting" weaponry. Throughout military history the primary objective of armed force has been to defeat the adversary's armed force, *not* to kill off the civilian population. But punitive, countervalue capabilities are demanded by the Mutual Assured Destruction theory, which U.S. military leaders, excepting a few, have tried to reject professionally even though forced to live with it politically.

This internal contradiction has resulted in the recent Pentagon proposals for basing the new MX missile. The MX is a counterforce weapon designed to destroy the most threatening of Soviet nuclear weapons before they are launched. It is the U.S. counterpart to the

Soviet SS-18 counterforce missile. As such, it is a militarily sound weapons system that could reduce damage to the United States. But the MX deployment schemes had to be compatible with MAD and its corollary arms-control premises. One scheme put forward in the Carter Administration and supported by the Air Force even into the Reagan Administration was the Racetrack plan which involved 200 MX missiles shuttled about among 4200 different shelters. A more recent proposal was MX Dense Pack which would have concentrated a hundred MX missiles in a huge slab of reinforced concrete for protection. These deployment schemes ran the cost of the $35 million MX weapon up to $300 million or more for each missile, the cost difference accounted by construction and reinforced concrete.

But it is not the cost that creates paradox. Because of enforced adherence to MAD, the deployment schemes for MX are designed to absorb the full weight of a Soviet attack *delivered by the same weapons the missile was designed to destroy before launch.*

The other option available to assure survival is to defend the country from nuclear attack. Instead of relying solely on the deterrent power of a punitive second strike, we can deter nuclear war by denying the horrible efficiency of a Soviet first strike against our country or our retaliatory forces. From every point of view—war avoidance, morals and ethics, military common sense, costs, timing, technology, and political reality—this is by far the best option available to us.

High Frontier maintains the long-neglected option of defending the United States from nuclear attack is viable. Not only is it possible to defend the nation against nuclear attack, it can be done so effectively that any first strike by the Soviets can be so severely filtered that the possibility of such an attack can be driven beyond the pale of credibility. We can change our strategy from Mutual Assured Destruction to Assured Survival and engineer an escape from the balance of terror we live in today.

First, though, one must make certain of what is meant by "defense." If effective strategic defense is defined as an impermeable shield through which no nuclear weapon could penetrate, there will be no defense. Obviously, no defense in history has ever been perfect—although this is precisely what the mid-sixties Secretary of Defense, Robert McNamara, demanded of any strategic nuclear defense. This sophistic absolutism was a key ingredient in McNamara's formulation of the MAD theory and has subsequently been the death knell of all proposals for active defense and civil defense for nearly two decades. An active defense was deemed implausible if it allowed any weapon to penetrate it. Similarly, a civil defense program was no good unless it saved everyone—and comfortably, at that. Saving three-fourths of our cities or 120 million of the 150 million American potential victims of nuclear war was not only deemed useless, it was deemed an extreme of cruelty to those who could not be saved! Consider the strange logic of the Australian, Mrs. Helen Caldicott and her Physicians for Social Responsibility who consider it immoral to make the slightest preparations to treat the sick and wounded should nuclear war occur.

High Frontier rejected absolutist demands on strategic defense and looked instead for defensive systems and programs which could add significantly to the U.S. deterrent to nuclear war. That is to say, High Frontier asked no more of strategic offensive systems than was asked of nuclear offensive programs such as Dense Pack. The proponents of Dense Pack could not make a case that all MX missiles so-deployed would survive, but they did make the case that Dense Pack would significantly increase uncertainty in the Soviet aggressor's mind that he could successfully conduct a first strike. That is all that High Frontier asked of strategic defensive systems—no more, no less than was asked of offensive systems.

In this light, defensive systems are more than competitive and more than cost-effective. In fact, for far less money and far more certainty than in the case of offensive deployments, defensive systems can destroy any confidence in the efficacy of a Soviet first strike.

As things stand today, the Soviets need only ensure that they can deliver two weapons of adequate accuracy and yield to destroy any target presented to them by additional offensive missile deployments. They have only to solve an arithmetic problem. If instead, the Soviets are presented with a strategic defense, they cannot determine in advance how many of their warheads will penetrate the defense, nor do they know which missiles will get through to damage which targets. Thus, the Soviet planner is no longer faced with a mere arithmetic problem but with a very difficult, if not insolvable, question. This alone indicates that we can do more to insure deterrence with a dollar spent on strategic defense than with one spent on improved offense.

Obviously, technology exists which can provide effective defenses for the United States quickly and at reasonable cost. High Frontier looked at dozens of systems and selected one set—not because they were the only technical solutions, but because these systems demonstrated how readily the strategic concepts of High Frontier could be supported by real U.S. capabilities.

No one should ever conclude that the systems selected by High Frontier are the only ones which will accomplish the strategic change we advocate. As a matter of fact, as will be discussed later, we believe that one system advocated in our original study may be second best to another we learned of a year later.

The fundamental military requirements necessary for a reincarnation of national defense are these:

—A spaceborne defense system capable of heavy attrition (fifty percent or more) of a Soviet long-range missile salvo against the United States in the early minutes of trajectory. The system must be available for deployment in the shortest time possible.

—A second layer of spaceborne defense, for later deployment, capable of inflicting further significant losses (another fifty percent or more) upon Soviet nuclear ballistic missiles which might escape destruction by the first spaceborne layer.

—A point defense of individual U.S. missile silos (MX or Minuteman) adequate to insure survival of those missiles long enough to allow them to be fired. This system must be quickly available, certainly before the MX missile is ready for deployment.

These three tiers constitute High Frontier's "layered defense" which can provide a ninety-six percent assurance of safety for all targets of Soviet long-range missiles and essentially one-hundred percent assurance of survival of our now-threatened land-based deterrent. Most of this could be accomplished by 1988, all of it by 1993. The so-called "window of vulnerability," which essentially is the threat to our land-based missiles from Soviet long-range missiles, can be closed in 1985.

In examining various available options to meet the three primary military requirements, High Frontier looked at a broad range of technologies which could provide the required defensive systems. This included weapon systems requiring nuclear warheads and weapons based on the emerging technology of beam weaponry—lasers, microwaves, and particle beams. It is important to note why these solutions were rejected in favor of simpler technologies.

The non-nuclear aspect of the systems favored by High Frontier is one of the concept's strongest selling points, but this is not a result from any bias in the team toward defensive nuclear weapons. Indeed, if there is one place where a nuclear weapon can be exploded without harm it is in space. Certainly, if nuclear explosions occurred in space to prevent other weapons from continuing their deadly course toward Earth, any ill-effects would actually be of tremendous advantage to mankind. If national defense against nuclear devastation could be best served by nuclear technology, High Frontier would advocate it despite the enormous political obstacles. High Frontier, rather, does not advocate nuclear systems for strategic defense because they are not the best military/technical solution. Spaceborne defenses, for one thing, require a large number of orbiting satellites, each armed with a great number of interceptor vehicles. Such defenses, would require more nuclear warheads than we now have in our entire stockpile. Secondly, any system employing nuclear weapons—whether in space or on ground—requires presidential approval for firing. Since defenses against ballistic missiles must react within a very few minutes of an attack, the necessary command and control systems associated with nuclear weapons could be crippling. Finally, technologies other than nuclear ones can disable Soviet missiles with equal or greater effectiveness.

Another rather remarkable aspect of the High Frontier military programs is that the key spaceborne defense system does not depend on laser beams or other futuristic weaponry. This fact was evident in the original study, but somehow friends and foes of the concept leaped to the conclusion that beam weaponry was a critical element in our recommendations. High Frontier stimulated a barrage of scientific and pseudo-scientific treatises on the technical and cost obstacles to space laser platforms. Others, although in great sympathy for strategic defense, assumed we were advocating some sort of "Buck Rogers" or "Star Wars" solution and became skeptical.

High Frontier, though, looked hard at beam-weaponry possibilites. Several of us—I, for one—started the search for technological answers convinced that lasers or some other beam weapon would emerge as the favored solution. That this turned out not to be the case should in no way suggest that such technology is not tremendously important or should not be pursued vigorously in U.S. research and development. Indeed, the High Frontier study strongly advocates this.

The advantage of a beam weapon over all others for spaceborne defenses is that the destructive power of such weapons moves at the speed of light. Theoretically, a space platform armed with a powerful beam weapon could destroy very quickly a large number of objects in space or even aircraft in the atmosphere. Certainly, the Soviets have been expending a great deal of treasure and energy to perfect such weapons. Their potential military value is too great for the United States not to guard carefully against a technological breakthrough in beam weapons.

The reason High Frontier's near-term proposals do not include such weapons is they do not meet time requirements. There are still too many technical unknowns in beam weaponry which will take much time to solve. There are many ideas as to perfecting such weapons for use on Earth and in space, but, outside laboratories, there is little practical demonstration or consensus among scientists on how to proceed.

We found the U.S. scientific community to be split many ways on the question of beam weaponry, the fundamental split between those who reject the idea of beam weapons in space entirely and those who believe them feasible. Some of the opposed appear to consult their politics more than their science when they deny any feasibility of beam weapons. They give themselves away by including lectures on "peaceful use of space" and the "arms race" in their critiques. Although the bias against all things military is evident among some scientific naysayers, there are indeed legitimate doubts about our ability to provide adequate power levels for such weapons in a small enough package to get into space, the ability to point and aim beams over vast space distances, and the complexity of a space vehicle capable of all this. The wiser scientists among the naysayers do not say it cannot be done; they only say it will take a very long time. As Dr. Edward Teller advises, scientists should be heeded when they say something can be done; they are often wrong when they say it cannot.

The High Frontier team generally rejected views of the doubting scientists and turned instead to those who said that spaceborne beam weapons were indeed feasible. There is a very respectable school of scientific opinion which holds that beam weapons capable of defending against Soviet ballistic missiles can be developed within the next eight or ten or fifteen years. A few scientists believe it can be done in as little as six years.

This was very encouraging, but we promptly found ourselves confronted with another dilemma. The "can-do" school of thought breaks into five warring camps when asked what kind of beam weaponry should be pursued. One group insists chemical lasers are the answer, a second opts for free electron lasers, a third for X-ray lasers, a fourth for no lasers at all, but microwave beams, and a fifth for instead a particle beam weapon. Suffice it to say that each of these approaches requires very different technological efforts and each, to bring results in a reasonable number of years, would require an expensive crash development effort.

Most of the team decided we could not confidently meet the military requirements of the High Frontier strategy, particularly as regards time, with lasers or other beam weapons. Clearly, it appeared that a national defense based on less exotic weaponry could probably be deployed before scientists resolved their arguments. However, we did conclude that beam weapon technology may be sufficiently in hand to constitute the basis for a second generation space defense.

One of the beam-weaponry proposals, the X-ray laser satellite, requires a bit more discussion. Here, is an example of a marvelous scientific idea which cannot stand the scrutiny of simple military logic. The X-ray laser operates by using the enormous quantity of Xrays produced by an exploding nuclear weapon, in this case contained in a specially designed chamber on a satellite. Parts of the tremendous energy generated by the explosion can be converted to laser beams which can travel along long rods extending from the satellite. If these rods (which would make the satellite resemble a sort of spaceborne sea urchin) can be pointed accurately at each of a large number of Soviet missiles, those missiles would be destroyed wholesale in an instant. While there are doubts about how to get all those rods aimed accurately at a myriad of targets at the instant of explosion, the supporters of this technology think it could be done. At any rate, the concept is certainly technologically "sweet," as the jargon goes these days.

Dr. Edward Teller, with whom we consulted frequently as High Frontier was being fleshed out, was particularly supportive of the X-ray laser option. The concept was in fact brilliant and appealed to him as a scientist. Further, it was based on a nuclear device, a fact which appealed to Dr. Teller as one of history's most eminent nuclear physicists. I do not think, though, that he has ever quite forgiven me for attacking this concept with the lowly logic of an infantryman.

Here is the rub. The X-ray laser, dependent

as it is on a nuclear explosion for power, must destroy itself to operate. If the Soviets should launch a single missile at the X-ray laser satellite, it could defend itself only by destroying itself, and then be unavailable to defend anything else.

These are some reasons why the High Frontier military programs are not very fancy. They are, in fact, based primarily on old technology and require the exertions only of engineers and scientists. This is one reason, no doubt, that High Frontier does not enjoy the enthusiastic support one might expect from members of the scientific community, some of whom have scoffed at the rather straightforward technical solutions of High Frontier as "scientifically unaesthetic."

The First Generation Spaceborne Defense

The High Frontier system chosen to illustrate the feasibility of spaceborne defense is the Global Ballistic Missile Defense I (GBMD I). This was the brainchild of Mr. Fred "Bud" Redding, then a conceptual engineer with Stanford Research Institute International. Redding's concept was never intended to dictate the final answer to the requirement for an early attainable spaceborne defense. Rather, it was designed to prove there was at least one way to get the job done in reasonable time with reasonable cost.

In coming up with GBMD I, Bud drew heavily, and wisely, on a massive amount of work completed twenty years ago by a strong Department of Defense scientific and technical team of over five-thousand. This group had concluded that even then it would have been technically possible to deploy a defensive system much like GBMD I within about six years, i.e., by *1968*! Bud applied the technological advances of the intervening two decades and concluded that the same kind of defense could be had now but with lower cost, greater ease and in less time. This straightforward, common sense approach is what has made GBMD I such a difficult concept to attack successfully, although attacked it certainly has been.

One key piece of information not available to defense scientists twenty years ago was the deployment pattern of the Soviet long-range missiles. Today though, that pattern of deployment is clear. Fortunately for the GBMD I concept, the Soviets have spread out their missile launchers and silos over their entire territory. In addition, the Soviet submarine-launched missiles are very long range ones which are just as profitable targets for GBMD as the ground-based missiles are. As a result of this dispersion, a satellite can be placed on orbit so as to be in position to intercept Soviet missiles on the rise for a good part of its hour-and-a-half journey around the Earth.

Of course, for a good deal of its orbit a satellite would be over South America, Australia, and elsewhere where it could not intercept a Soviet missile. (Perhaps more importantly it would often be over Libya, Red China, and Cuba where it might also have to be used.) In order to at all times keep enough satellites in the right position to detect a Soviet attack and engage the hostile missiles, a rather large number of satellites would be required. Furthermore, we need enough satellites to permit them to defend each other, if necessary, from an enemy attempt to interfere with the defensive system. In the case of GBMD I, 432 such satellites are required. Analysts from other organizations have recommended a smaller number, 200 to 300 satellites, but of larger size.

These satellites would be put in orbit 300 miles above the Earth by the Shuttle (which can carry 12 or more at a time) or by ordinary booster rockets. The size of the GBMD satellite was selected, in fact, so that it could be put in orbit by the MX booster. These satellites could stay in orbit indefinitely, since at that height we expect no orbital decay—i.e., gradual falling back to Earth. But they are expected to become inoperable due to technical malfunction of some sort after five years in orbit. They would then be replaced.

These satellites would consist essentially of a frame, a computer, a sensor, a communications package, a rocket motor, and forty to fifty small rockets capable of intercepting Soviet missiles. The brains of the satellite—its computer—must know precisely where it is in space at all times in order to launch its interceptor rockets accurately to engage the targets. This is not as difficult as it may sound for, once the orbit is established, the satellite's path is established with such little variability that precise location as a function of time is rather easily programmed.

The satellites are fairly simple as satellites go, so much so that High Frontier refers to them as "trucks." These trucks keep a constant vigil over near-Earth space—from the Earth's surface up to about 500 miles. They would detect a Soviet missile salvo about 1000 miles ahead, track the missile to determine the point in space where it can be struck by interceptor missiles and then pass that information to the other trucks. When any truck's computer calculates that one or several of its interceptors can make one or more kills, it automatically dispatches them to the appropriate points in space.

The interceptor is, like the rest of the system, not very fancy. Its job is to take off at high speed from the truck toward a designated point in space. It has its own sensor which can pick up the target shortly before impact and can maneuver very slightly with small steering rockets to improve accuracy. It is highly likely that this interceptor can actually ram itself into the Soviet missile. The DOD team of twenty years ago believed this kind of system would achieve only a one or two-foot miss distance. But just to make sure the interceptor made its mark, it would create a cloud of "buckshot" some twenty-five feet in diameter just prior to impact.

The Soviet missile would obviously suffer catastrophic damage if just one of these pellets struck it. It would be kinetic energy which destroys it. The formula for this is: energy equals mass times velocity squared ($E = \frac{1}{2}MV^2$). The velocity of the truck is 17,000 miles per hour. The velocity of the interceptor is added to make the pellets strike at about 20,000 miles per hour. With such great velocity, the mass need be very small to impart a tremendous amount of energy on the target. In fact, an ice cube hitting a Soviet missile—or any other object in space—at such speed would destroy it. Inhabitants of Kansas or other tornado prone areas have seen straws driven into telephone poles by this same principle of kinetic energy.

In a normal, peacetime situation, GBMD I would be under positive control by the "man in the loop" at all times. This is necessary since the system operating on fully automatic would shoot down cosmonauts, scientific probes, and missile tests. The information gathered and processed aboard the trucks on orbit will constantly be passed to a U.S. or allied ground authority from the trucks in the system passing over the Earth-based space defense headquarters. This would almost certainly be the large, hardened facility inside Cheyenne Mountain at Colorado Springs. In times of no special tension, the GBMD system would not engage any target unless instructed to do so by that authority.

In periods of higher, but non-critical world tension, the entire system could be semi-autonomous. A threshold of numbers of launches from hostile territory could be established, beyond which GBMD I would automatically engage targets. In other words, in a period of tension we might wish to accept the risk that some few missiles might be allowed to proceed without interception by the defense, even if fired at our satellites, but we would want maximum efficiency against a heavy nuclear attack. Such maximum efficiency comes when the system is autonomous.

In a crisis period such as the Cuban Missile Crisis, the GBMD would be placed on full alert and would fire autonomously on every missile rising from hostile geography. This would mean notification to the Soviet Union—and others capable of space launches—that we could not, in light of the situation, consider any launch as peaceful. This autonomous mode hopefully would never have to be implemented, but the capability to implement it is essential to maximize its deterrent value and to minimize the vulnerability of the system's satellites and those key reconnaissance and communications satellites already on orbit and so vital to our security.

The GBMD could, of course, shoot down our own missiles as well as anyone else's. This would not happen though because the computer banks aboard the GBMD trucks would contain the data necessary to prevent it. But for those seriously concerned about accidental nuclear war, GBMD's ability to destroy the errant nuclear missile is important. While the "madman military officer" *a la Dr. Strange-love* seems farfetched (and insulting too, since he is usually conceived to be an American, never a Russian), the possibility of a fanatic such as Muammar Khaddafi or the Ayatollah Khomeini creating this kind of situation is not diminishing but growing as nuclear weapons proliferate. GBMD would remove such triggers for all-out nuclear war.

This in a nutshell, is GBMD I. It is non-nuclear. You would not hurt a soul on Earth with it—no part of it could reenter the atmosphere. And, it uses mostly old technology, obtained quickly and at reasonable cost. It would allow us to escape the failed MAD theories, thus protecting us from nuclear attack.

Nevertheless, GBMD has been and will be attacked relentlessly from many quarters.

Second Generation Spaceborne Defense

GBMD I will begin to reduce the confidence of any Soviet general who might contemplate a first strike against the United States or our allies when the first of these defensive satellites are deployed. In five or six years, the full system could be in orbit, capable of destroying fifty to eighty percent of a missile attack as it rises out of the Soviet Union and surrounding seas. But this is not good enough for the long haul.

GBMD II is a follow-on system which utilizes more advanced technology to strengthen, perhaps replace, GBMD I. It is designed to extend the time during which the nuclear missiles can be destroyed *from the first seven minutes after launch to the full half hour it takes them to reach the atmosphere over the United States*. Its objective will be to destroy eighty percent of all warheads that get through the first layer (GBMD I) so that from ninety to ninety-six percent of any Soviet long-range missile salvo will be destroyed en route.

Since we do not expect this second generation of spaceborne defense to be designed for seven to eight years or deployed before ten years, there are many more options available to us, perhaps some we have not yet heard of.

Two types of emerging technology seem most likely to constitute the basis for a second generation space defense, one being beam weaponry discussed earlier, the other improved sensor technology which would make the basic GBMD I system effective throughout the trajectory of an ICBM.

One problem with beam weaponry is vulnerability. Beam weaponry satellites, we believe, would be large, complex, costly and few in number. Thus, they have vulnerabilities not shared—or shared only to a much lesser degree—by the GBMD I. However, with GBMD I in place a great deal of protection is provided for the beam weaponry platform, enhancing its survivability. It may well be that the scientists who prefer the truly high technology answers over the "scientifically unaesthetic" GBMD I may find that the ugly duckling has its virtues after all.

Be that as it may, there is a strong chance that beam weaponry will make its debut as GBMD II in the early nineties, though which of the various types of beam weaponry will emerge is still hard to tell.

The advancing technology most likely to form the basis for GBMD II is an advance in sensor technology. GBMD I uses sensors that pick up the heat of a rising missile in contrast to the very cold background of space (four degrees above absolute zero). This easily-detected contrast weakens as the missile stops burning its engines and cools off. For this reason, GBMD is effective only in the early stages of a missile's trajectory. But we know how to detect the much weaker contrast between a manmade object such as a cooled-down missile, satellite or reentry vehicle and space. The Air Force anti-satellite (ASAT) weapon currently being developed has to do just that. As a matter of fact, the ASAT uses the same principle as the GBMD except that its target is an enemy satellite rather than a missile. But the Air Force's ASAT must be carried to near-space by an airplane and then launched at its target since the ASAT's sensor must be supercooled cryogenically in order to spot the target. We do not yet know how to manufacture this kind of sensor in a way that would allow us to put it in orbit for five or six years and expect it to function when needed. Hence, we cannot engage Soviet missiles throughout their trajectory with GBMD I.

If this sensory problem could be solved, either by improving cryogenically-cooled sensors so they can live in orbit for several years or by developing another type of sensor altogether, GBMD II could be essentially an upgrade of GBMD I. This might occur by adding improved satellites to GBMD I or simply by replacing GBMD I satellites with more capable ones as their life in orbit expires. Such an option would most certainly be the least expensive way to implant GBMD II in Earth-orbit. Boeing Aerospace engineers have estimated that GBMD II could be had for a mere $5 billion add-on to the cost of GBMD I.

Ground Defense

For those of you who feel more comfortable on the ground than in space, High Frontier includes some down-to-Earth recommendations. These include defending our missile silos from Soviet missile attack with machine guns—yes, I said machine guns—and that long-neglected function Civil Defense.

High Frontier estimates that it will take five or six years to deploy the first layer of space-borne defense, GBMD I. If it were possible to acquire GBMD I in half that time, we would not have bothered to recommend a ground-based third tier of active strategic defense. The spaceborne system can by itself destroy any Soviet confidence in the effects of a first strike against our deterrent, and thus close the "window of vulnerability." But we need to close that window sooner than in five to six years.

Further, we would not have bothered to recommend a ground-based defense if we could not have found a system that could be effectively and cheaply deployed in two or three years. A quick-fix between the current vulnerability of the U.S. deterrent and its future protection by a space-based defense was deemed necessary. But it would indeed have to be deployed quickly, unlike the ten-year MX Racetrack Program, the six-year B-1 program or the six-year ground-based ballistic missile defense program which had been developed by the Army.

We sought a system which would quickly remove any real or presumed confidence the Soviets might have in their emerging capability—announced by Secretary of Defense Harold Brown in 1979—to destroy the bulk of our land-based missiles. We wanted to find a system that could carry the full weight of closing that window of vulnerability for a few years only, and then be relegated to the far simpler task of defending against Soviet missiles which might penetrate GBMD I.

By sharply limiting the mission of a ground-based defense we were able to find solutions that were indeed cheap and quick. All current and previous Army programs for anti-ballistic missile defenses have been based on defending a large area—say an entire missile field. This meant that the ABM system had to be able to intercept any Soviet reentry vehicle which might fall anywhere within the defending area. This in turn meant catching the enemy warhead six or eight miles up after sorting out decoys from real warheads. This required very advanced, very expensive, and very vulnerable radars. The main components of these area-defense ABM systems become of themselves highly lucrative targets for Soviet attack and much of their complexity and cost was due to the need to defend themselves.

High Frontier rejected this classic approach to ballistic missile defense. We sought a defensive system that would do nothing more or less than defend the one U.S. missile silo to which it was assigned, against only those warheads threatening the silo, and for no longer than was necessary to get the missile launched. The system was to be as different from previous concepts as defending an airfield is from providing a tailgunner for a bomber. All the High Frontier ground-based system really had to do was sit close to the silo to be protected, with simple radars stare perpetually up that rather limited cone of atmosphere through which a warhead must travel to reach that silo, and destroy the first two or three warheads to arrive.

And, we found such systems. One is the SWARMJET, described in some detail in the original High Frontier study. It utilizes simple range-only radars to detect the incoming warhead and predict an intercept point. A large number (a "swarm" of thousands) of small, non-explosive rockets are then fired to intercept the incoming warhead about one kilometer from the silo. If the warhead explodes (and it is by no means certain that it would) the exposed radar dishes and the SWARMJET launchers would be destroyed. Replacements would pop up from underground to take on the next incoming warhead. (The rest of the radar would be permanently underground in a silo of about the same hardness as the protected missile.)

Since publication of the High Frontier study, we have found that the same mission can be performed with a rapid-fire, Gatling-type gun. General Electric has perfected this thirty-millimeter gun and is already supplying them in quantity to the U.S. Air Force and the Dutch Navy. This gun, the GAU-8, has been tested, with astonishing results, against a simulated Soviet reentry vehicle. If a slug from this gun hits the reentry vehicle it destroys it. A pair of these guns firing at a reentry vehicle provide an almost one-hundred percent assurance of destruction before the reentry vehicle can get close enough to a current Minuteman Missile silo to damage it.

We could start deploying this kind of defense around our missile silos now. It would cost about $10 million per silo to install such a defense, and for one-hundred MX missiles in old Minuteman silos, that amounts to $1 billion. Contrast that with the $20-60 billion required for other solutions to MX deployment! Too, we can deploy defenses for the vulnerable Minuteman, Titan and/or the new MX missile faster than new missiles can become available. We can defend the entire ground-based missile force against a first strike for half the money proposed for protecting only one-hundred MX's in Dense Pack.

Remember this: we can adopt this quick and relatively inexpensive approach to defending our missile silos only if we look downstream to the other, spaceborne defense element. Given five or six years, the Soviets could probably find a way to overcome the simple point defense. The point defense and space defense are not readily separable ideas. Those who, for various reasons, oppose High Frontier also oppose taking this first step of point defense.

Finally, on the ground and readily do-able, is Civil Defense. It has been apparent for decades, despite the terror-mongering of the disarmament lobby, that Civil Defense could save millions in a nuclear war. Unfortunately, some champions of Civil Defense also attempt to frighten their fellow citizens into action.

The future of Civil Defense is inexorably intertwined with the future of strategic defense as a whole. The slogan "There is No Defense" will never become "There is No Defense except Civil Defense". Until the MAD theory is discarded, in action as well as words, Civil Defense will remain a withered arm.

V.
The Non-Military
High Frontier Programs

"Tapping the unlimited sources of material and energy in space may be the most important agenda point for this civilization for the next 100 years."
–Dr. Peter Glaser

President Reagan, in his 1983 State of the Union message, maintained the United States needed to exploit the "new frontier of high technology." There is not better way to put that wise advice into action than to adopt High Frontier as national strategy.

A little-discussed but vitally important aspect of High Frontier is the opening up of space for maximum industrial and commercial use. Space-borne military capabilities and space industrialization go hand-in-hand. The core technology required to support one, supports the other. Security from destruction, seizure or other interference in space commercial enterprises must be government provided for private industry to be willing to risk fortunes on outer-space's high frontier.

Government must do for the space frontier what it has effectively done for other frontiers: explore, assist in building transportation systems, and provide security. The United States has already explored the solar system. It has put men on the Moon, sent mechanical explorers to distant planets, explorers that return astonishing photographs of the rings of Saturn and Jupiter. It was the government which developed transportation systems from the great Saturn booster to the Shuttle. Government has yet to provide the security required in space for private investment; it is as yet insufficiently supportive of private industry in space.

Yet space has been one of the few areas of government spending which has been a boon to private industry and commerce. Today, thanks to the space effort, we have a thriving micro-electronics industry, a half-billion-dollar-a-year space communications industry which may grow to a $20 billion-a-year industry in 1990. Even the stick-free pans in many American kitchens were an offshoot of the space program. For every tax dollar put into the space program, six have been returned to the economy.

There are eight hardware programs recommended by High Frontier. Three are the all-military programs already discussed. The other five programs are, to varying degrees, partly military, partly non-military—a fact which underscores the silliness of the current wave of propaganda about militarizing space.

The non-military programs address two primary interests for private industry in space. One is improved transportation and the other is pilot programs to increase commercial opportunity. These ideas are closely interlinked. Commercial applications in space become viable in direct proportion to the reduction of the cost-per-pound to orbit. So long as the cost per pound in orbit is at one-thousand dollars, nothing that is worth less than one-thousand dollars per pound is going to be transported in space—rare pharmaceuticals, yes; perfect silicon crystals, perhaps; ball bearings, no.

For this very reason, transportation systems are high among priorities for High Frontier. The Shuttle, remarkable as it is, is the DC-3 of space transportation. The Boeing 747 of space is down the line somewhere. We should be trying hard and investing much to produce the new generations of spacecraft. The Advanced Space Shuttle is one possibility. Another is the High Performance Space Plane, a utility craft with many applications and capable of going anywhere in space with a one-man crew. This craft or one like it would, of course, be helpful to both military and civilian, space operations. This particular one is designed to be launched from the back of a 747 and change orbits by skimming back down to the atmosphere to avoid the heavy fuel requirements needed normally to change orbits.

One transportation link which NASA has unsuccessfully been trying to get funding for is a space port—the Space Operations Center (SOC). Such a port would accommodate industry development and testing of commercial space applications. On the military side, the SOC would serve as the space-deployed arm of the Space Command in Colorado. A secure alternate command post for control of the space military systems, including GBMD, the Space Operations Center would be permanently manned, providing docking facilities for the Shuttle, the High Performance Space Plane, and for yet another vehicle, the Space Tug or orbital-transfer vehicle needed to move men and materials even further into space.

Finally, there is High Frontier's program for government encouragement of industrial space development.

Space is a unique environment which will permit us to create valuable products impossible to profitably manufacture on Earth. Space provides a near-perfect vaccum— something which only can be achieved at great cost here on Earth. Space also provides a zero-gravity environment which, except for brief moments, cannot at all be achieved on Earth. Space is free of germs (except those brought up inside an astronaut's space suit) and is thus a completely sterile environment, something achievable only at great cost in a few hospitals and laboratories. Space, at only four degrees above absolute zero, provides unlimited heat absorbtion ("heat sink" in technical jargon) so that industrial problem of heat generated by a manufacturing process need not be absorbed by the atmosphere, streams, and the sea to the detriment of our environment. Space is also an unlimited source of materials and energy which, on Earth, are in short supply.

On the fourth flight of the Space Shuttle Columbia, one experiment was a prelude to the first manufacturing plants in space. In this experiment, extremely valuable pharma-

79

ceuticals were separated from other chemicals in a process unable to be performed on Earth. This was a joint venture by the pharmaceutical company Johnson and Johnson and the aerospace company McDonnell-Douglas. It will eventually become possible to produce, in space, large quantities of such wonder drugs as interferon which has shown remarkable results in treating cancer but which can only be produced in minute quantities on Earth. And, this is but the beginning of possibilities for American industry should we get serious about opening up and securing the high frontiers of space.

One of the most exciting possibilities is utilization of the sun's inexhaustible energy supply for electricity on Earth. There is absolutely no technical obstacle to this, as a joint NASA-Department of Energy research project has proved.

The NASA Solar Power Satellite (SPS) operates from a geosynchronous orbit 23,500 miles above the Earth. There it is forever in sunshine as it remains at all times over the same spot on Earth. This satellite consists of millions of solar cells, which convert sunlight directly into electricity, and an antenna which converts this electricity into microwaves (much like those that carry our TV signals) and beams them to

Earth. On Earth, a large receiving antenna converts the microwaves back into electricity which is fed directly into a power grid. A laser beam in the center of the receiving antenna is aimed to the center of the sending antenna in space, keeping the two locked firmly together at all times. The system is environmentally benign, posing no hazard to life on Earth. Aircraft, birds, and butterflies can fly through the beam without risk.

One such satellite can generate as much electrical power as five coal-burning or nuclear plants—enough to provide electricity for large metropolitan areas such as New York or Tokyo. We would for once be adding to Earth's resources rather than depleting them. The SPS would tap directly the same source of power that we now tap so indirectly when we burn fossil fuels. And, unlike our current sources of energy which cost dearly to extract and transport, the cost of the fuel for the SPS is zero.

There are places in the world today where the struggle to produce enough fuel to cook food and stay warm is creating social and environmental disasters. In some less-developed nations, little girls spend most of their daylight hours not playing or learning, but patting cattle dung into balls and setting them out to dry as fuel for the village stoves. Elsewhere, whole mountain ranges are denuded of every stick of wood as big as a man's finger. This leaves bare hills brings and on catastrophic erosion, floods, and the destruction of wildlife habitats.

Energy from the sun could be delivered to such areas and move them from Stone Age agriculture to rural electrification without the necessity to first create the complex infrastructure of ports, roads, rail lines, power plants, and skilled labor forces required by other solutions to their engery deficiencies. All that would be required is the receiving antenna and power lines.

By 1980 we knew that such a system for tapping power from space was technically possible. As our scientists develop more efficient solar cells and other pertinent technologies, solar power satellites become an evermore attractive option for meeting the growing energy needs of Earth. Machines necessary to build such large space structures automatically have in fact already been developed.

Despite the fact that solar power from space is unquestionably technically feasible, it is not being pursued by the government. The drawbacks are vulnerability and cost. If today we had such satellites in orbit, they would be subject to interference or even destruction by a hostile power. Neither governments nor private industry are likely to commit the tens of billions of dollars necessary for an unprotected and fragile spaceborne power plant. Thus, the military protection of high frontier's total strategy constitutes a critical element in the future of spaceborne power generation.

Today, the costs of a solar-power satellite system are too high to make it competitive with construction of additional coal-burning and nuclear power plants in advanced industrial states. Ironically, SPS power costs are competitive with other kinds of power generation in under-developed countries where neither the fuels nor the necessary infrastructure exist to introduce or expand coal-burning or nuclear power plants. These countries, of course, have no capability whatsoever to create a spaceborne solar power system. A further irony is the fact that many of the underdeveloped countries, for political reasons, advocate a crippling obstacle—the United Nations Space Laws. Such efforts would create barriers to the exploitation of space similar to the inhibitory influence of a international Law of the Sea on the exploitation of the sea bottoms. This political "solution" would deny the technologically advanced nations any realistic opportunity to tap these resources for the benefit of all people.

The high costs of the SPS are primarily a function of the cost of transporting the necessary men and materials to geosynchronous orbit. Thus, the future of energy from space is heavily dependent on the High Frontier non-military efforts to improve space transportation and reduce the costs-per-pound to orbit. Meanwhile, however, there must be an active and vigorous research effort to make certain that the United States and the Free World shall stand ready to exploit this enormous potential for the improvement of the human condition.

VI.
The Naysayers

*"There is no bias as strong
as the bias toward what you were
saying and doing yesterday."*
–Anonymous Bureaucrat

Diligent bureaucrats in the Departments of Defense and State, in the Arms Control and Disarmament Agency, and elsewhere in government have been working over the past fifteen years or more to perfect programs and policies to support the MAD theory. When High Frontier challenges that theory, applecarts are upset all over Washington. To accept High Frontier is to accept the unwelcome news that much of the bureaucracy—in and out of military uniform—has been plowing in the wrong field for more than a decade. Small wonder then that, inside government, the tendency has been to seek ways to squelch rather than ways to support new concepts.

Outside government, High Frontier poses a serious challenge to a large confederation of activists—including groups that are anti-defense, pro-disarmament, anti-technology, world government idealists, out-and-out proponents of Marxism, and the mere faint of heart. Objections to High Frontier from this quarter are sometimes disguised as a questioning of technology and costs and are sometimes undisguised political polemicism.

The general thrust of criticisms of High Frontier from inside and outside government are outlined below with the responses thereto:

"The technology required to implement High Frontier is not off the shelf. In fact, there are serious technical risks in the proposal for a spaceborne defense."

This is a fading category of objection and already a far cry from earlier charges of "defying the laws of physics." Our scientists and engineers have responded effectively to specific criticisms. However, the most telling fact is that the GBMD I system was deemed technically feasible by a DoD team of scientists and technicians twenty years ago.

Some critics have referred to High Frontier's GBMD I as "BAMBI Revisited." BAMBI (Ballistic Missile Boost Intercept) was part of Project Defender which was the research effort ordered by President Eisenhower in 1959 to determine the feasibility of defenses against intercontinental ballistic missiles. By mid-1962 this effort included twenty of DoD's best scientists and engineers backed by five-thousand support personnel. This team concluded that a non-nuclear, kinetic energy kill, spaceborne defense system, almost identical in concept to High Frontier's GBMD I, could have been deployed by 1968 at a cost of thirty billion 1962 dollars. This was a remarkable result when one realizes that the computers available at that time were rather primitive, using cathodes and diodes, which means that the proposed defensive satellites had to weigh up to ten times more than those proposed by High Frontier. The only available booster which could carry such large satellites to orbit was the Saturn which later launched our astronauts to the Moon. The expected mean-time-to-failure of satellites (their probable useful life in space) was eighteen months as opposed to the five years or more of today's satellites. The BAMBI team did not have a clue to the probably distribution of the Soviet ICBM launchers since none had yet been deployed. They predicted (correctly) that there would be phenomenal increases in our ability to handle data with a commensurate decrease in required weight to orbit and (again, correctly) that the cost-per-pound to orbit would sharply decrease.

One can, I suppose, make the case that the BAMBI team consisted of a lot of lotus-eaters talking nonsense. The reputations of the men involved are a rebuke to that dodge. The fact is that bright and audacious men knew how to create High Frontier's required systems two decades ago. The rebuke must be for today's government technocrats, armed with dramatic increases in the required technologies and a precise knowledge of Soviet missile deployments and characteristics, who raise doubts about feasibility.

An aspect of High Frontier that should give pause to any who would challenge it on technological grounds is the caliber of the team itself. The Chief Scientist was Dr. Arnold Kramish, a nuclear physicist who worked in the Manhattan Project during World War II. Our expert on ballistic missile defense was Major General Stewart Meyer, who had headed the Army's BMD effort at Huntsville, Alabama for three years. Other prominent scientists who worked on the project were Peter Glaser, father of the solar-power-satellite concept and J. Peter Vajk, eminent physicist and space expert of Livermore Laboratories. This is to name but a few. The men and women who contributed to High Frontier were not lotus-eaters either, nor were the score of Boeing Aerospace engineers who scrubbed down High Frontier's technology and found it sound.

One curious aspect of challenges to High Frontier on technical grounds is the lack of specificity in the charge. When the High Frontier team has been able to pinpoint areas where there is allegedly substantial technical risk we have found the objection rather easily answered. For instance, when early objections to technical feasibility of High Frontier's GBMD I turned out to be Defense Department doubts about the availability of laser weapons, we had only to point out that they are not used in GBMD I.

"Well, even if it is technically sound, High Frontier's spaceborne systems will cost far more than you say and take a lot longer to achieve."

The cost and time-to-deploy arguments are completely interdependent. The High Frontier team contends that GBMD I can be deployed in five or six years at a cost of about $15 billion. Early on, these figures were challenged with offhand estimates of "about the year 2000 to deploy, at a cost of $200-400 billion." I know of no one who cares to support this view of cost and timing with the possible exception of one man in the President's Science Advisor's office and Admiral Larocque's

Center for Defense Information, an offshoot of the pacifist "Fund for Peace." The former Deputy Secretary of Defense, Mr. Carlucci and Dr. Eberhardt Rechtin, President of Aerospace Corporation, are on record with an estimated deployment of a High Frontier-type system in ten to twelve years at a cost of $50 billion.

The DoD-Aerospace figures are, in our view, correct. And they are about the same as those of the Boeing Aerospace experts. They are correct if one assumes business-as-usual in system acquisition. Our incredibly inefficient acquisition procedures, now accepted as normal, have resulted in thirteen-year efforts to acquire military aircraft, three times as long as industry takes to produce a new commercial aircraft of equivalent complexity. Government and industry authorities agree that about thirty-percent is added to the end cost of a system for each year the acquisition process is stretched out beyond the actual time required for development and production. Our figure of about $15 billion in five to six years is based on special management of a Manhattan Project type to get results efficiently. The costs would certainly be inflated to $50 billion if the time for acquisition is doubled to accommodate bureaucratic inertia and red tape.

We have not always been saddled with cumbersome and costly acquisition procedures. The most advanced aircraft in the world today, the SR-71, was obtained in two-and-a-half years; the Polaris submarine, with far more technical risks than High Frontier's GBMD, was obtained in forty-seven months; and we landed on the Moon in seven years from a go-ahead. This was possible because either we had not yet introduced today's tangle of bureaucracy into our procurement and acquisition system or clever men found a way to circumvent it.

In 1956, President Eisenhower ordered the building of a totally new, technologically risky weapon system, the Polaris, and got it in 1960. In 1970, Richard Nixon ordered a product improvement to Polaris, the Trident submarine. Three presidents later, in 1981, we got one. Such is the radical decline in efficiency which carries with it a tripling of costs. With business as usual, High Frontier's time and cost schedules cannot be met. With management arrangements recommended in our study, ones which worked in the past, they can be met.

One way to evaluate the cost of High Frontier is this: Currently it costs us somewhere between $50 million and $250 million per U.S. satellite in orbit. The most expensive of these satellites are the highly complex models such as our reconnaissance vehicles which push state-of-the-art technology to its utmost and require expensive precision placement in orbit. High Frontier's satellites (or "trucks") would certainly fall in cost toward the lower $50 million end of the scale since they are relatively simple and do not require precision insertion into orbit. High Frontier's satellites—within our $15 billion estimate—cost $36 million each, or in the DoD estimate about $100 million per satellite. High Frontier would require five-hundred identical satellites and thus a production-line effort to produce them. Current satellites are hand-tooled and custom-built, with only a handful of any one type ever constructed. Unit costs are enormous, with each satellite bearing a large chunk of research and development expenditure. Economies of scale would certainly push the costs down toward our figure.

Objections to High Frontier on cost considerations fail to address the savings which it would permit elsewhere in defense expenditures. High Frontier would protect one-hundred MX missiles deployed in our old Minuteman silos for $1 billion worth of the point defense systems proposed. Compare that with the $20 billion in Dense Pack or $60 billion in MX-Racetrack for concrete and construction alone. There is also a necessary $20 billion for hardening of the U.S. command, control, and communications system to withstand the full weight of an unfiltered Soviet missile attack, and to rebase our SAC bombers. Much of that would be unnecessary if High Frontier were pursued. High Frontier will not add to defense expenditures, it will reduce them.

High Frontier, by destroying the rationale for a Soviet first strike against our current retaliatory forces, restores their original value. Our older offensive systems, Minuteman missiles, B-52 bombers, and Polaris submarines in port, would retain their value as a deterrent if they could not be destroyed in a Soviet first strike. Thus, much money already spent by the American taxpayer would once again contribute to our strength and our deterrent. And this does not even take into account the billions saved by protecting our conventional forces from attack.

High Frontier is a global defense concept. It defends not only America, but our allies in Europe and the Pacific as well. It is therefore perfectly reasonable that our allies could be expected to help pay for High Frontier either directly or in offsets to other U.S. defense costs.

Finally, the surge of growth in the high

technology sector of the economy which would be sparked by a U.S. commitment to High Frontier will more than offset its costs. In fact, space has proved the best investment our government has made over the past two decades. The expenditure of about $5 billion per year to pursue the civil and military programs of High Frontier will not only ensure our security but will result in a net profit. High Frontier is a strategic bargain of immeasurable worth.

"The trouble with High Frontier is the vulnerability of space systems. The Soviets will figure out a way to blow a hole in GBMD and then fire their missiles through it."

From the inception of Project High Frontier, survivability was recognized as a key issue. Early on, some Air Force notables opined that spaceborne defensive satellites were an attractive idea but "they will shoot them down as fast as you put them up." This reaction had a familiar ring to it. It is almost precisely the doubt of Army generals in the early 1900s when it was suggested that aircraft be used in combat. Largely because of concern for vulnerability, the Army concluded at the time that the utility of aircraft was confined to communications and reconnaissance and thus, aircraft were duly assigned to the

Signal Corps—which is basically the status of spacecraft in today's military.

As a result of concern for spacecraft survivability, Project High Frontier devoted more time to analysis of this issue than of any other issues raised by the concepts. Basically, the approach was to confront High Frontier's defense system with every conceivable type of threat—from throwing sand in the path of satellites to speculative, exotic, Soviet beam weapons (including a few in the classified category). We considered so-called peacetime attacks as well as wartime attacks. While we certainly did not conclude that our system concept was invulnerable, we found no readily available or confidently attainable Soviet threat which would render GBMD ineffective. Each threat became manageable through a combination of technical or operational countermeasures. Further, we found that the GBMD of High Frontier was the best single answer to the dangerous vulnerability of U.S. satellites already in space and so vital to our security.

When viewed piecemeal, i.e., in terms of an individual defensive satellite against a given postulated Soviet threat, the survivability picture in technical terms looks indeed bleak. However, when the total defense system is confronted with the same threat, the survivability problem eases dramatically. The GBMD concept is remarkably survivable relative to other spaceborne systems because of the numbers of vehicles, their relative simplicity, and their ability to defend one another from direct ascent threats. In this respect, the large number of vehicles required by a kinetic energy kill system constitutes a distinct survivability advantage over a system consisting of relatively few beam weapon kill vehicles.

Most important is the strategic reasoning behind the deployment of a spaceborne defense in the first place. Its primary strategic purpose is to deter a Soviet first strike. The purpose is not to survive, not to prevent a Soviet retaliatory strike, and not to totally eliminate the Soviet missile threat. When this basic fact is borne in mind, it is clear that even if the Soviets devise means to knock a hole in the satellite system to launch an ICBM attack on the United States, they could not expect a first strike to succeed. They would never believe that after such an assault on our defense systems, our offensive weapons would await destruction on the ground. Thus, even if one postulates an effective Soviet attack against GBMD, it would not destroy the basic strategic reason for deploying it.

It should also be noted that some of the postulated Soviet counters to GBMD involve massive investment and long lead times. For instance, one study suggested that the Soviets might mass their ICBMs in a small piece of geography in order to bore through the defense. That is a physical possibility, of course, but it is fraught with adverse strategic considerations for the Soviet planner. It would cost enormously and would take a decade to even partially accomplish. And, again, the Soviet first-strike threat would be negated for the foreseeable future.

"The big problem with High Frontier is not technology or costs, it is the effects of it on arms-control, especially the ABM Treaty."

We expected a good deal of concern about the effects of High Frontier on the ABM Treaty and devoted considerable space to the issue in our study. But we have found, as we traveled the country, that it is not an issue with the public or the press. Curiously, we hear most about it from the Pentagon. Secondly, we have found the public is highly supportive of defense against Soviet ICBMs. A recent poll showed that two out of three Americans believe we already have a defense against ICBMs; eighty percent said they want such a defense and that cost would not be a primary factor in their minds.

Finally, it may well be, as some arms control buffs now say, that reasonable agreements with the Soviets will become possible only when defensive weapons are reemphasized. Consider this. If the United States adopted the High Frontier recommendations, our arms-control negotiators could make a proposal to the Soviets along these lines:

"The most destabilizing of weapon systems on both sides are long-range ballistic missiles. Only by using these weapons could either side ever hope to carry out a successful first strike against the other's homeland. We have declared that we have no intention of delivering a first strike against the Soviet Union, but perhaps you do not consider that an adequate guarantee on which to base the security of the Soviet Union and the Socialist Bloc. If nothing else, your heavy expenditures on strategic defenses and civil defense indicate this. You have also stated you have no intention of launching a first strike against the United States, but we can reasonably doubt that such a declaration is adequate to insure the security of our country and our allies, especially in light of your deployment of first strike weapons such as the SS-18 missile.

"We are going to deploy a purely defensive, spaceborne defense to insure that we cannot be subjected to a nuclear first strike by any nation or combination of nations. It will be a non-nuclear system which cannot possibly be used for attack of any person on earth. We invite you to deploy a similar system to prevent any nuclear first strike against the Soviet Union. We believe our current treaty arrangements should be amended to make it quite clear that these bilateral steps toward a stable strategic situation are mutually acceptable. We are willing to agree to measures which will ensure that the systems deployed are unmistakably defensive and non-nuclear.

"If we can both look forward to the day when neither side must constantly guard against a first strike on our retaliatory forces and our nations as a whole, then surely we can actually reduce the total numbers of nuclear weapons on both sides, as President Reagan has proposed."

This kind of arms-control offer has some chance of success. It is not based, as U.S. arms-control efforts thus far have been, on the hope of creating more balance in the balance-of-terror, as required by the Mutual Assured Destruction Theory, but on creating a situation of Mutual Assured Survival. Total nuclear weapon stockpiles would be effectively reduced by applying technology which makes the accumulation of offensive nuclear weapons less important to both parties.

True, the Soviets may very well reject the entire proposal. But by doing so, they would declare themselves unwilling to accept any solution which denies them first strike capability against the United States. Thus, we must proceed with High Frontier whether or not they agree to work for Mutual Assured Survival.

"If we choose to reemphasize strategic defenses, how do we know that the Soviets will not quickly deploy a lot of ABM's?"

We don't. I, for one, am convinced that the Soviets have been preparing for a breakout in ABMs ever since the ABM Treaty was signed. If the United States moves to deploy space-borne defenses and this were to cause abrogation of the ABM Treaty, there is a strong possibility that the Soviets would begin an extensive deployment of ground-based ABMs.

However, one must then ask: So what? The Soviets would be adding to strategic defenses they already have; we would be creating a strategic defense where we had none. Our problem is our vulnerability.

Certainly the Soviets could, over a number of years—and at the expense of resources which are now being spent on more offensive capability—deploy enough ABMs to further weaken the effectiveness of our deterrent threat. But, with a vigorous U.S. effort to deploy the High Frontier defense systems, the strength of our deterrent will grow faster as its elements are made ever more survivable.

The final attack on High Frontier is an attack on the basic strategy. It is essentially the old "defense is destabilizing" argument. It goes like this:

"If the United States moves to defend itself against the most powerful element of the Soviet nuclear arsenal, the Soviets will view it as preparation for attack, and will attack us to prevent it."

Strangely enough, we get this argument most often from people who have in the past condemned pro-defense spokesmen as paranoid when they voiced concern about Soviet advantages in strategic nuclear power allowed in SALT II. The arms-control enthusiasts then insist the Soviets are in such mortal terror of the destructive power of a few Polaris subs that they would never use their offensive advantages. The real vexation for such people is that High Frontier offers a solution to our strategic dilemmas that is quite independent of the agreements and arms-control treaties with the Soviets which have long been their sole solution. High Frontier denies the apocalyptic vision which, it is easy to see, is the foundation of the entire pacifist, nuclear freeze movement.

We must squarely face the full import of accepting this kind of objection. If we conclude that we cannot deploy a non-nuclear defense system which cannot kill a single Russian on the grounds that it might be too irritating to the Kremlin, we are accepting the proposition that America can never again be defended. We would condemn future generations to live constantly in the menacing shadow of a balance-of-terror, a balance certain to favor those states most likely to use terror to gain their ends.

We should reject objections based on fear of Soviet reaction even if there were a palpable possibility of violent Soviet reaction. The fact is that such a Soviet reaction is too remote to weigh on the decision. The idea that strategic defenses are destabilizing is the odd notion of American so-called Defense Intellectuals. That idea is utterly rejected by the Soviets, as indicated in this reply to a newsman by former Soviet Premier Kosygin:

> "I believe that defensive systems, which prevent attack, are not the cause of the arms race, but constitute a factor preventing the death of people. Some argue like this: What is cheaper, to have offensive weapons which can destroy towns and whole states or to

have defensive weapons which can prevent this destruction? At present the theory is current somewhere that the system which is cheaper should be developed. Such so-called theoreticians argue as to the cost of killing a man—$500 thousand or $100 thousand. Maybe an anti-missile system is more expensive than an offensive system, but it is designed not to kill people but to preserve human lives. I understand that I do not reply to the question I was asked, but you can draw yourselves the appropriate conclusions."

This is but one example of the oft-stated Soviet refusal to accept the premises of Mutual Assured Destruction, particularly its rejection of strategic defense. The Soviets refer to such ideas contemptuously as "bourgeois naivete." And you need not take their word for it. Over the past decade or so, the Soviet Union has spent more on strategic defense than we have on strategic offense. For every ruble they have spent on strategic offense, they have spent one ruble on defense against nuclear attack. The United States, on the other hand, has spent one dollar on strategic defense for every ten-thousand spent on offense.

High Frontier's successful defense of our concepts has had some good effects. For one thing, the original tendency to scoff is rarely in evidence now. Further, Secretary Caspar Weinberger has voiced his support for the basic concept in public, to wit: "What is really needed is the development of a new ballistic missile defense system, based in space, that can destroy incoming missiles before they even get into the atmosphere." President Reagan, in early July 1982, voiced some basic support with his remarks about the "ultimate frontier" of space. In his January, 1983 State of the Union address, he extolled the "new frontier of high technology." The High Frontier, though, will never become a reality through the recommendations of bureaucrats whose turf it threatens. You can be assured that when political leadership decides the new strategic direction, the technical, cost, and time arguments will disappear overnight within the bureaucracy.

Still, they will not so readily disappear from the rhetoric of the ideological opposition. The Left, until recently, has refrained from direct attack on High Frontier. They were hopeful, it appears, that bureaucratic obstinacy would do its work for them. In early 1983, under the leadership of Congressman Joe Moakley of Massachusetts, the ideological assault on High Frontier was launched. Moakley is sponsoring, along with other members of the House of Representatives—Dellums, Weiss, Mikulski, Frank, etc., (a literal who's who on the Left)—a resolution forbidding any and all U.S. weapons in space.

Whether Moakley and his colleagues realize it or not, this resolution is in direct support of a Soviet effort in the United Nations to ban all space weapons, an effort launched a few weeks after the first Shuttle flight.

The *Congressional Record* contains Mr. Moakley's assault on High Frontier, which he dubs "high foolishness." He includes a diatribe against High Frontier by Dr. Bowman who amply cites objections from unnamed Pentagon critics. Nothing could more effectively demonstrate the tacit alliance between the anti-defense spokesmen on the Left and the all-offense proponents in the Department of Defense. Both insist that "there is no defense" and "there should be no defense."

At about the same time Moakley and Company launched their attack, a new Institute for Security and Cooperation in Outer Space was founded in Washington. It was presided over by a young man named John Pike, one-time advisor to presidential candidate Barry Commoner. Its objective: defeat High Frontier. Its primary tactic: attach anti-High Frontier objectives ("no weapons in space") to the nuclear freeze movement's list of demands. According to Mr. Pike, this new institute's funds are to come primarily from the Rockefeller Family Fund.

The "Center for Defense Information," a deceptively named organization in the anti-defense, pro-unilateral disarmament, nuclear freeze coalition, has also launched an attack on High Frontier. Retired Rear Admiral Gene Larocque, its hired chief spokesman, attacks High Frontier on the grounds of cost, while making it perfectly clear that he would oppose defending America from space if it could be done free.

The Left really had no choice but to oppose High Frontier. It constitutes an effective counter to the nuclear freeze movement around which the Left has been rallying and reviving the old McGovern coalition. Mr. Moakley and Admiral Larocque know that High Frontier can appeal to the bulk of Americans, especially to young Americans. Both these men know it must be defeated if the Left is to avoid a large defection of frightened Americans swept into the nuclear freeze movement.

The political battlelines are now pretty well drawn. If we are to take advantage of our opportunity to once again defend America, the political battle must be won, and won now.

VII.
In Sum...

The United States and its allies now have the combined technological, economic, and moral means to overcome many of the ills that beset our civilization. We need not pass on to our children the horrendous legacy of "Mutual Assured Destruction," a perpetual balance of terror that can favor those most inclined to use terror to bring down our free societies. We need not succumb to ever-gloomier predictions of diminishing energy, raw materials, and food supplies. We need not resign ourselves to a constant retreat of free economic and political systems in the face of totalitarian aggressions. The peoples of the Free World can once again take charge of their destinies if they but muster the will to do so.

In April of 1981, the Space Shuttle Columbia made its dramatic maiden voyage into space and returned safely to Earth. This event was not merely another admirable feat of

American space technology, but rather it marked the advent of a new era of human activity on the high frontier of space. The Space Shuttle is a development even more momentous for the future of mankind than was the completion of the transcontinental railway, the Suez and Panama Canals, or the first flight of the Wright brothers. It can be viewed as a "railroad into space" over which will move the men and materials necessary to open broad new fields of human endeavor and free us from the brooding menace of nuclear attack.

This is an historic opportunity; history is driving us to seize it.

A few thousand years ago, man's activities—his work, his commerce, his communications, all of his activities including armed conflict—were confined to the land.

Eventually man's technology and daring thrust his activities off the land of the continents and into the coastal seas. His work, commerce, communications, and military capabilities moved forcefully into this new arena of human activity. Those nations that had either the wit or the luck to establish the strongest military and commercial capabilities here reaped enormous strategic advantages. For example, the Vikings, although never a very numerous people, became such masters of the coastal seas that their power spread from their homes in Scandinavia over all the coasts of Europe and into the Mediterranean and up to the very gates of Byzantium.

At the beginning of the sixteenth century, after the epic voyages of men like Magellan and Columbus, human activity surged onto the high seas. Once again, the nations that mastered this frontier reaped enormous strategic rewards. First, Spain and Portugal utilized sea power to found colonies and to solidify their strength in Europe. Later, Great Britain, with an unsurpassed fleet of merchantmen and fighting ships, established a century of relative peace which we remember as Pax Britannica.

In the lifetime of many of us, man's activity moved strongly into yet another arena, the coastal seas of space—the air. And once again, the nations which quickly and effectively made use of this new arena for commerce and defense gained tremendous advantages. As Americans, we can take pride that the greatest commercial and military successes in aviation were achieved by our own nation which provided us over thirty years of confident security.

But today, following the epic voyages of our astronauts to the Moon and our unmanned explorer satellites to the rings of Saturn and beyond, we find man's activities moving strongly into yet another new arena—the high seas of space. Already the United States and other major nations, including the Soviet Union, are making huge investments in outer-space. Much of our communications, intelligence, weather forecasting, and navigation capabilities are heavily dependent on satellites. And, as history teaches us, those nations or groups of nations that become pre-eminent in space will gain the decisive advantage of this strategic high ground.

We must be determined that these advantages accrue to the peoples of the Free World and not to any totalitarian power. We can improve the Shuttle, our railway into space, placing space stations at its terminals and sharply reducing the cost-per-pound of material put into space. We can thus open the doors of opportunity to develop entirely new space-based industries, promising new products and new jobs for our people on Earth. We can eventually create the means to bring back to Earth the minerals and the inexhaustible solar energy available in space. By doing so, we can confound the gloomy predictions of diminishing energy and material resources on Earth. This will not only enhance the prosperity of the advanced, industrialized nations of our Free World, but will also provide solutions to many hitherto intractable problems of developing countries.

Further, we can place into space the means to defend these peaceful endeavors from interference or attack by hostile powers. We can deploy in space a purely defensive system of satellites using non-nuclear weapons which will deny any hostile power a rational option for attacking our space vehicles or for delivering an effective first strike with ballistic missiles. Such a global ballistic missile defense system is well within our present technological capabilities and can be deployed in space, in this decade, at less cost than other available options.

We need not abrogate current treaties to pursue these defensive options. A United Nations treaty prohibits placement of weapons of mass destruction in space, but does not prohibit defensive space weapons. The ABM treaty requires discussion among Soviet and U.S. representatives of any decision to proceed with defensive systems "based on other principles" such as space systems. We should initiate such discussions and propose revisions, if necessary, in the ABM treaty which is now scheduled for review.

Essentially, this is a decision to provide an effective defense against nuclear attack for our country and our allies. It represents a long overdue concrete rejection by this country of the "Mutual Assured Destruction" theory which held that the only effective deterrent to nuclear war was a permanent threat by the United States and the Soviet Union to heap nuclear devastation on the cities and populations of each other. The inescapable corollary of this which (perhaps the most apt acronym ever devised in Washington) was that civilian populations should not be defended, as they were to be considered hostages in this monstrous balance of terror doctrine. The MAD doctrine, which holds that attempting to defend ourselves would be destabilizing and provocative, has resulted not only in the neglect of our active military, strategic, and civil defense, but has also resulted in the near-total dismantlement of strategic defenses we once had.

For years, many of our top military men have decried the devastating effect MAD has had on the nation's security. In fact, our military leaders have, over the years, denied its validity and tried, within the limits of their prerogatives, to offset its ill effects. But those effects are readily evident. The only response permitted under MAD to increased nuclear threats to the United States or to its allies was to match these threats with increased nuclear threats against the Soviet Union. Further, a U.S. strategy which relied at its core on the capability to annihilate civilians and denied the soldier his traditional role of defending his fellow citizens has had a deleterious effect on the traditional American military ethic. Indeed, it has effected the relationship between the soldier and the normally highly supportive public.

This legacy lies at the heart of many current security problems. We should abandon this immoral and militarily bankrupt theory and move from "Mutual Assured Destruction" to "Assured Survival." Should the Soviet Union wish to join in this endeavor—to make Assured Survival a mutual endeavor—we would, of course, not object. We have an abiding and vital interest in assuring the survival of our nation and our allies. We have no interest in the nuclear devastation of the Soviet Union.

If both East and West can free themselves from the threat of disarming nuclear first strikes, both sides will have little compulsion to amass ever-larger arsenals of nuclear weapons. This would most certainly produce a more peaceful and stable world than the one we now inhabit. And, it would allow us to avoid bequeathing the horrendous legacy of a perpetual balance of terror to future generations.

What we propose is not a panacea for all national security problems. Spaceborne defense does not mean that our nuclear retaliatory capabilities can be abandoned or neglected. The United States would still maintain strategic offensive forces capable of retaliation in case of attack. The Soviets, while losing their advantage in first strike capabilities, would still be able to retaliate in the utterly incredible case of a first strike by us. Nor does our approach to the strategic nuclear balance eliminate the need to build and maintain strong conventional capabilities.

We Americans have always been successful on the frontiers; we will be successful on the new high frontier of space. We need only be as bold and resourceful as our forefathers.

If you would like additional copies of *We Must Defend America*, please use the order blank below and send it along with your check to:

HIGH FRONTIER

1010 Vermont Avenue
Suite 1000
Washington, D.C. 20005

1 — 50 copies	$2.95 each
50 — 100 copies	$1.95 each
100 — 500 copies	$1.45 each
500 + copies	$ .99 each

Enclosed is my check for _____ copies of *We Must Defend America*.

Please send to:

_____
Name

_____
Address

_____
City   State   . Zip

_____
Phone #

Please make checks payable to High Frontier.

If you would like additional information on High Frontier please fill in the request below and send to:

High Frontier
1010 Vermont Avenue
Suite 1000
Washington, D.C. 20005

Please send information about High Frontier to:

_____
Name

_____
Address

_____
City   State   Zip

THE WHITE HOUSE

WASHINGTON

June 3, 1983

Dear Dan:

It was very kind of you to dedicate your book
to me. I appreciate the important work that
you and your colleagues have done to prepare
the way for a more secure America.

You -- and all those who have made the High
Frontier project a reality -- have rendered our
country an invaluable service for which all
future generations will be grateful. I value
greatly your continuing efforts to help us
build a national consensus and to find the
difficult answers for the profound strategic
problems that face all of us in this nuclear
age.

God bless you!

Sincerely,

Ronald Reagan

Lt. General Daniel O. Graham, USA, Ret.
High Frontier
Suite 1000
1010 Vermont Avenue, N.W.
Washington, D.C. 20005